How to Make patterns with thread

How to

Make patterns with thread

D. Neville Wood

photographs by Stanley Ackroyd

Studio Vista

Studio Vista, a division of
Cassell & Collier Macmillan Publishers Ltd.,
35 Red Lion Square, London WC1R 4SG
Sydney, Auckland, Toronto, Johannesburg
an affiliate of Macmillan Inc., New York

Filmset and printed by BAS Printers Limited, Wallop,
Hampshire

First published in Great Britain 1974

ISBN 0 289 70442 1

Contents

Introduction

First, a word about the title. I like to call these patterns 'filametric'. And you will not find the word in a dictionary because I made it up.

Sometimes these patterns are called 'mathematical needlework', even though many of them involve very little maths, and often it is just not needlework at all!

More often it is called 'curve stitching'. But, although it is true that the illusion of curves is created, most of the lines are dead straight. And it is not always 'stitching'. 'Thread sculpture' seems equally misleading, and 'nail-and-wire pictures' is too restricted a description.

My home-made title combines the ideas of a fine thread like the filament of a lamp and measurement: hence 'filametric'.

The patterns are easy to make and the variations are endless. This new hobby, which is becoming very popular with both children and adults, will cost you little more than a few pence and some patience. Later on, when you design your own patterns and ways of using this new skill, you will be able to create attractive wall-panels, table-mats, 3D models and unusual gifts.

This book will take you, step-by-step, through the early stages of a fascinating hobby.

D.N.W.

Materials

To begin with, all you need is:

good quality plain paper (typing or cream-wove writing
   paper is fine)
fibre-tip pens (crayons or ball-point pens will do, or
   even a well-sharpened pencil)
ruler (preferably clear plastic)
pencil and soft eraser

Later on you will need:
a pair of compasses
clear plastic protractor (preferably a 360° protractor)

**When you become more ambitious you may need
some of these:**
veneer pins or panel pins (tiny nails) or gimp pins
lurex thread, string, or other fancy wools or threads,
   or even thin wire
felt or coloured hessian
polystyrene tiles

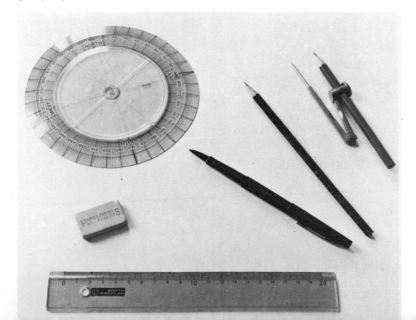

Drawing simple patterns

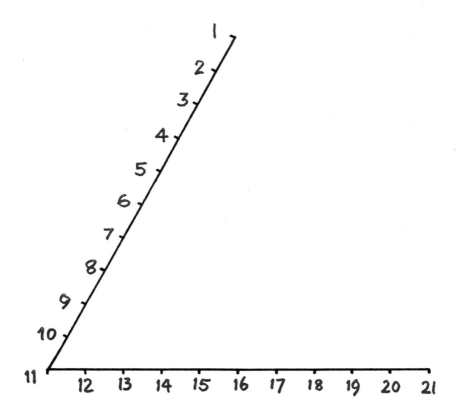

A simple 'curve'

Draw a straight line 10 centimetres long. Mark it off in divisions of 1 centimetre.

Draw another line at an angle of about 60° to the first one and mark this off in the same way.

If your ruler is marked in inches, make the lines 5 inches long and the divisions half an inch apart. So long as you make the lines the same length as each other, and the number of divisions remains the same, the actual unit of measurement is unimportant.

Lightly pencil in the numbers from 1 to 21 as shown.

With the ruler, draw a line from points 1 to 12

2 to 13
3 to 14
4 to 15
5 to 16
6 to 17
7 to 18
8 to 19
9 to 20
10 to 21

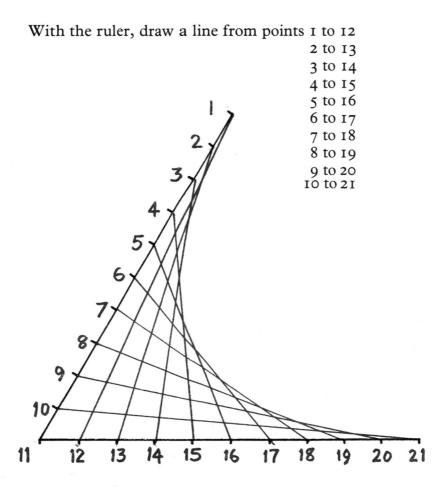

Rub out the pencilled numbers. You have now completed your first pattern.

The curve or parabola is not really a curve at all. You know that it is made up of straight lines.

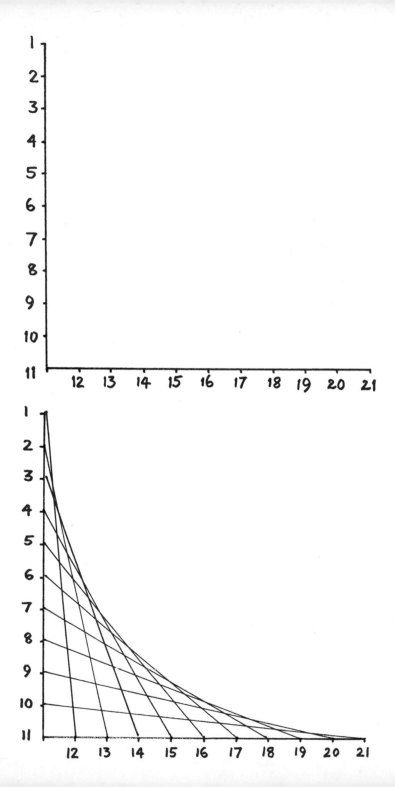

Try the same pattern again, but using a different angle. The one on the facing page is 90°, or a right angle.

Use the same numbering, and the same joins:

1 to 12	6 to 17
2 to 13	7 to 18
3 to 14	8 to 19
4 to 15	9 to 20
5 to 16	10 to 21

Now look back to page 9. You will see that the different angle has made a different curve.

You could try a pattern with an obtuse angle (larger that 90°) – 120°, perhaps, or even 135° – and notice the difference in the result.

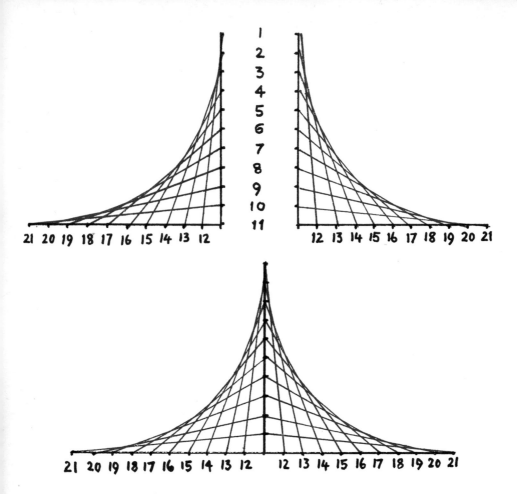

'Reflections'

Try drawing the right-angle pattern the other way round, to make a mirror image or reflection. You could even put them back-to-back.

If you have a clear idea of which points join, you can soon begin to rule your patterns without the numbers. Take care not to miss out one of the 'points' as you move your ruler round. This is where you will discover the advantage of a clear plastic ruler over a wooden or metal one.

You could make a 'reflection' in another direction.

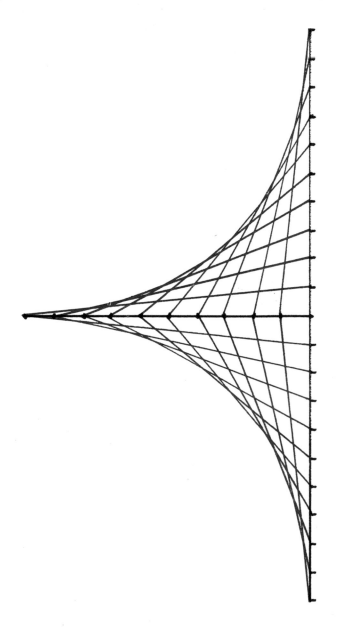

You will probably be able to complete these straight-forward patterns without numbers by now.

The next step is to bring all four right-angle patterns together.

Here is the grid which you should mark out first on the paper.

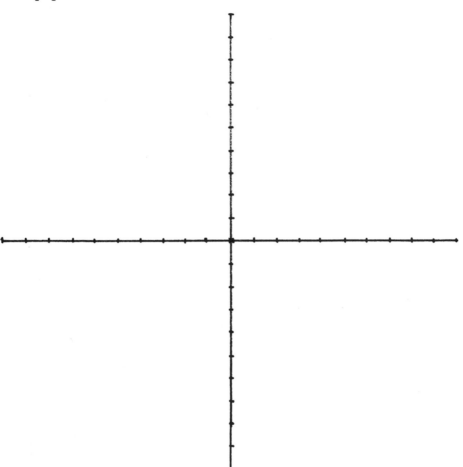

If you can manage without the numbers, so much the better. Remember that the actual length of the lines, or axes, is unimportant so long as, at this stage, they are the same length as each other. The divisions marked off along the axes must be equal in number and spaced equally along them.

And here is the finished result of four right-angle patterns together.

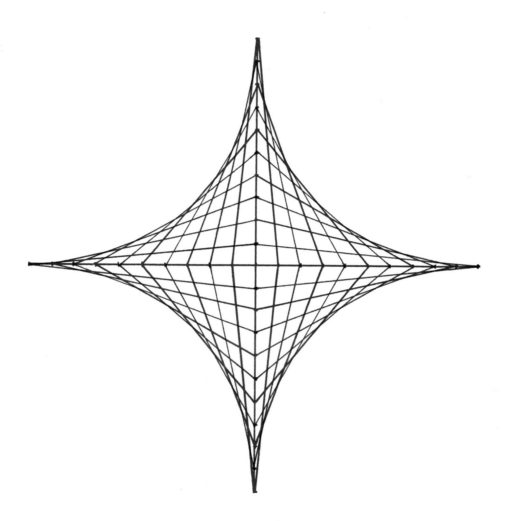

Try as many colour combinations and variations as you wish. You will create striking results if you choose two contrasting colours for alternate lines.

Straight lines make a circle

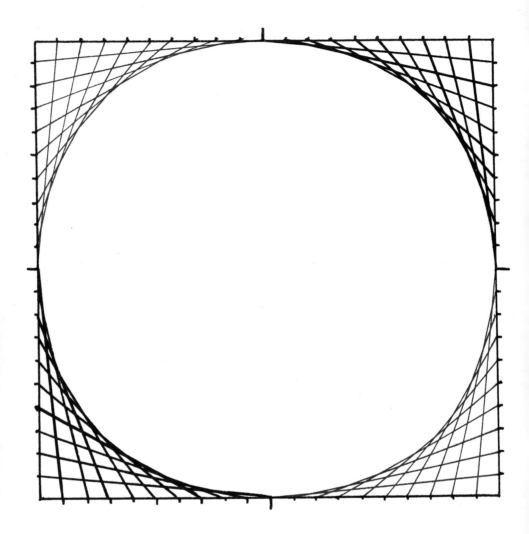

How can you draw a circle with a ruler? By joining four 'curve' patterns.
It's long-winded, but it works.

The green pattern on the cover was made like this, but using lurex thread and nails (see page 26).

You could fit these four corner patterns on top of each other.

Two different colours have been used for this diagram to help you see which points to join.

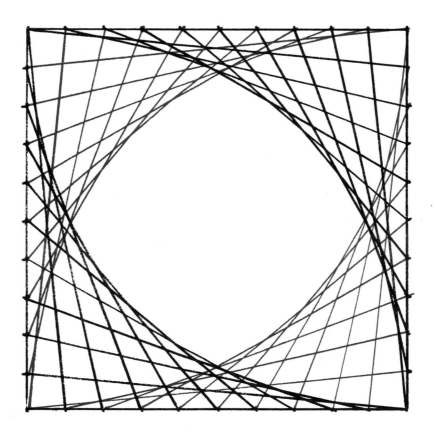

If you prefer, you could use all one colour, or you could use a different colour for each corner; or any other variation you like.

Drawing patterns in a circle

Six-point circle

It does not matter how many points you mark out around the edge, or circumference, of the circle, as long as they are equal distances apart. The easiest is the six-point circle.

Draw a circle with your compasses. Without altering the angle of the compasses, use them to mark off six points round the circumference.

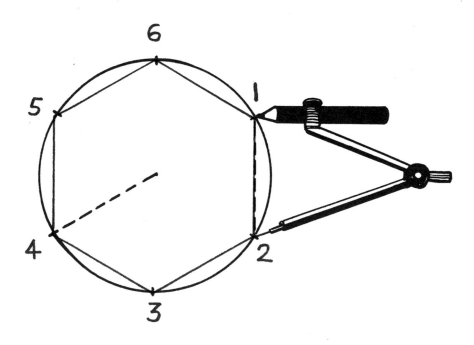

You could join 1 to 2, 2 to 3, 3 to 4, and so on. This will give a hexagon.

Or you could join all the diameters,

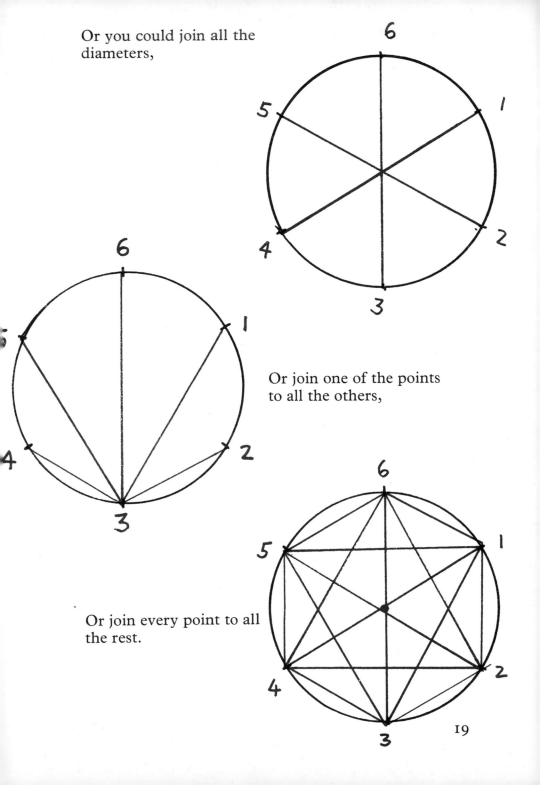

Or join one of the points to all the others,

Or join every point to all the rest.

Twelve-point circle

You can mark off the circle into as many sections as you like.

This one has been marked off into 12 equal parts (30° on the protractor). Each point was joined to every other point.

Some people call this design the Mystic Flower or Mystic Rose.

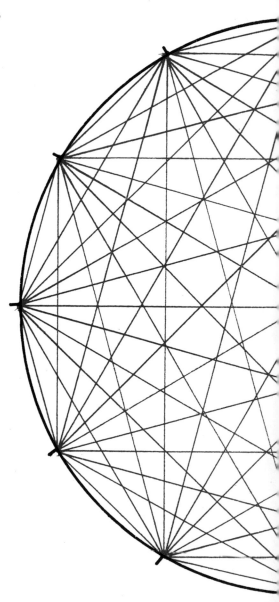

How many lines do you have to draw for this pattern? Can you count them, or will you have to work it out by arithmetic?

The pattern on page 34 was made like this, but with 24 points instead of twelve. (Just think how many lines must make that up!) It was made on a nail-board instead of drawn. On page 26 you will find out how.

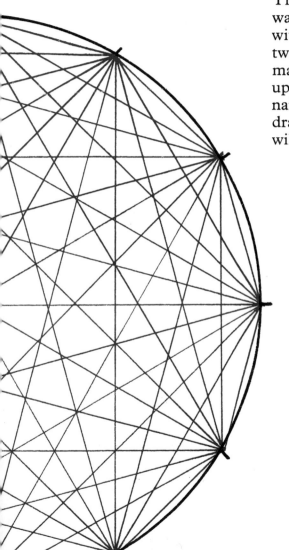

Stitched patterns

You need:
a piece of thin card *or* a
    polystyrene tile
protractor
gimlet or knitting needle
ruler
needle and fancy thread (or
    wool, thin string – or
    anything you can sew
    with)
ready-gummed paper
    spots (these are not
    essential)

1 Stick the paper spots
onto the tile. This one has
twelve spots – 30° apart.
If you do not have paper
spots, mark the numbers
onto the back of the tile.

2 Number the spots like a
clock. Make a hole with
the gimlet or knitting
needle next to each spot.

3 Thread the needle
and start stitching.
Bring it up through 12,
leaving a long end, then
down at 5, up at 6

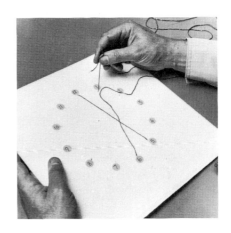

down at 1, up at 2
down at 7, up at 8
down at 3, up at 4
down at 9, up at 10
down at 5, up at 6
down at 11, up at 12
down at 7, up at 8
down at 1, up at 2
down at 9, up at 10
down at 3, up at 4
down at 11.
Tie the ends at the back.

This will give you the
finished design. You can
now peel off the numbered
spots.

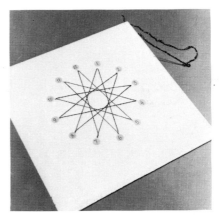

Saving thread

Any of the designs in this book may be stitched. But you should work out the sequence of stitching carefully so that you cover all the lines you need without wasting thread. This design was drawn on page 9. This is the order of stitching:

up through hole 1,
down through 12, up at 13
down through 2, up at 3
down through 14, up at 15
down through 4, up at 5, and so on.
You will end up going down through 10.

If you want to stitch the angle, printed in black on the diagram, do it in this order:

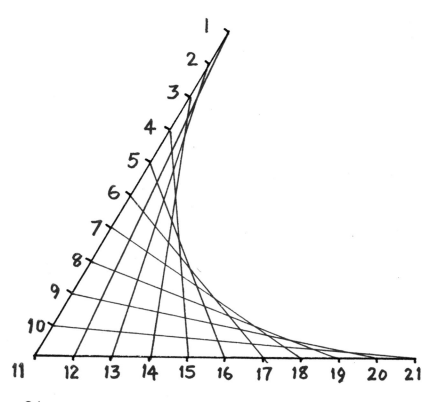

after going down through 10, come up at 11,
down at 12, up at 13
. . . . and so on, until you come up at 21.
 Now work back again, going down at 20, up at 19,
down at 18, and so on.
Stitch the other side of the angle in the same way.

Using polystyrene tiles

Here are some suggestions for displaying designs
stitched on polystyrene tiles.

1 Pin them to a wall or ceiling with dressmaking pins.

2 Glue a plain tile on the back with special cement.
These would make pretty table mats for a special
occasion.

3 Glue another stitched tile on the back.

4 Pin six tiles together to make a cube. They could all
have the same design, or all have different ones. Or you
could mix plain tiles with patterned ones. You could use
it as a free-standing decoration or, as it is so light, you
could hang it from a thread to make a mobile.

Using nail-boards

Making a nail-board

You need:
a piece of plywood 1 cm thick
    (or chipboard or good quality insulation board. Do
    not use hardboard)
panel pins or veneer pins (tiny nails)
hammer (a small toffee-hammer is best)
pencil, ruler, compasses, protractor,
fancy thread, wool, string, or wire

 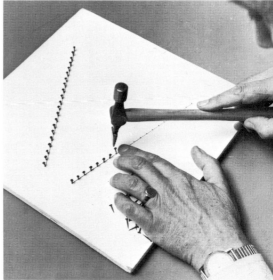

You could give the board a coat of emulsion paint first, but this is not essential.

Whatever kind of pattern you are going to make, this is the way to start.

1 Draw the angle, lines, or circle on the board with pencil.

2 Mark the positions where the nails are to be. It does not matter how wide apart they are, but they must be evenly spaced.

3 Hammer the nails firmly into the board, but not all the way in. Make sure you hammer them all in to the same depth.

Circles on a nail-board

This nail-board will be used for patterns based on a circle.

The circle can be as large or as small as you like. You can use as many or as few nails as you like. The important thing is that the nails should be evenly spaced.

The great advantage of using a board like this is that you can undo the pattern, change it round, or use different colours, just as you please.

This circle has 36 points. The thread was moved on 13 points each time.

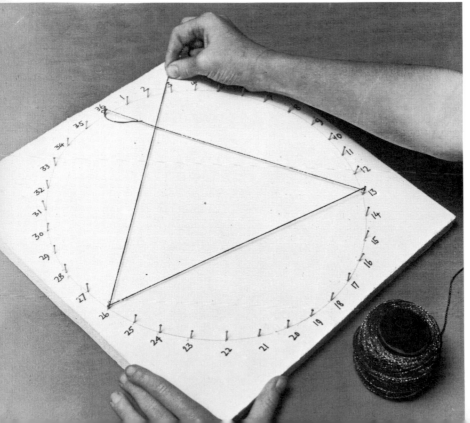

You could also make a nail-board using a square shape.

Drawing an ellipse

To be really unusual, you could use an ellipse, or oval. This is how to draw one.

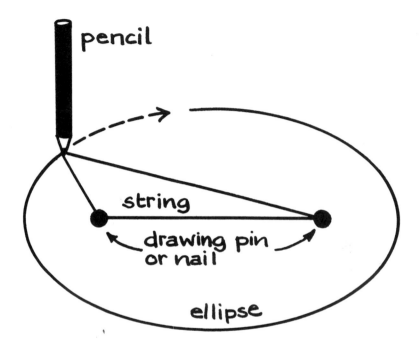

1 Hammer two nails into a board.

2 Cut a piece of string about three times as long as the distance between the two nails. Tie the ends together.

3 Fit the string loop round the nails. Holding the pencil upright, use it to pull the string loop out tight. Draw the ellipse, letting the string guide the pencil. Be careful of the knot in the string. It will make the pencil 'jump' if you do not move it out of the way.

Using a nail-board

It is easy to use a nail-board. Instead of taking the thread through the base as you do when stitching, you wind it round the nails.

This is how to make the angle pattern on page 9.

Tie the thread to nail 1. Take it across to nail 12, give it an extra turn round nail 12, pulling it tight.

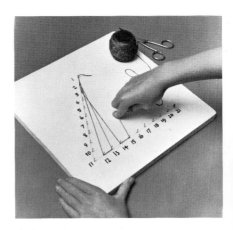

Now take the thread to nail 13 and wind it round. Then to nail 2, nail 13, nail 4, nail 15, nail 4 . . . and so on until you have finished the pattern.

To fill in the spaces, weave the thread in and out of the nails along each angle – or wind it round each nail as you go.

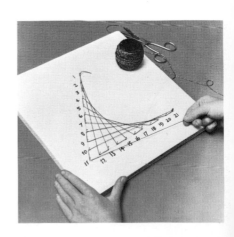

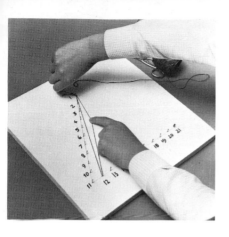

You could make this same design another way. Each of the lines will be made up with a double thread.

If you want to avoid filling in gaps at the end, this is the sequence to use.

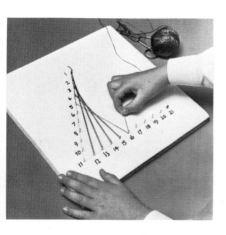

1, 12, 13, 12, 1
2, 13, 14, 13, 2
3, 14, 15, 14, 3
4, 15, 16, 15, 14
5, 16, 17, 16, 5
6, 17, 18, 17, 6
7, 18, 19, 18, 7
8, 19, 20, 19, 8
9, 20, 21, 20, 9
10, 21, 10
11, 12, 11, 10

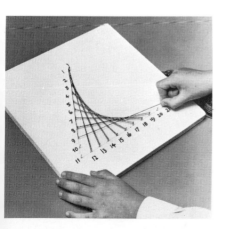

You could make an even more impressive design using six of the triangles described on page 31. They all have an angle of 60°.

The black lines are the ones to draw first. They should all be the same length. Each line should have the same number of nails and all the nails should be evenly spaced, as before.

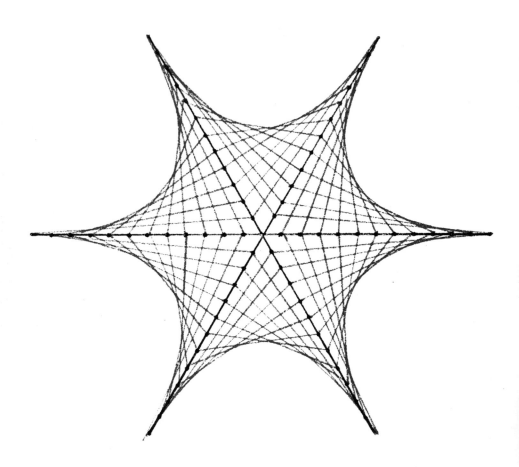

Opposite This pleasing design is made up of two right-angle curves (see page 11), a thirteen-point circle, and a thirty-six point circle. Notice how the colour of the wood and the painted nails add to the design.

Extra hints

If you want to make a 'fan' effect or a Mystic Flower pattern (see page 20), remember that the nails will be taking quite a strain with the number of turns of wire or thread that they will be holding. It would be best to use stronger nails, possibly 2·5 cm (or 1 in) wire nails.

If you wish, you can touch up the heads of the nails with coloured paint. Use gold or silver paint if you are using lurex thread, or else use a colour that will blend or contrast with the colour of the base board. In this way the nails can form part of the overall effect.

Instead of painting the base board, you could cover it with coloured paper, or perhaps metal foil, like the Mystic Flower design on the facing page.

Opposite : A Mystic Flower design (see page 20) using 24 points and several colours of thread on a base board covered with metal foil.

Below opposite : A design stitched on cardboard, using obtuse angles and 'reflections' (see pages 11–12).

All on a simple square

This section will give you some idea of the different patterns you can build up on a square. .

You can draw these patterns, or stitch them (see page 22), or make them on nail-boards (see page 26).

Try using a 10 cm square marked off in 2 cm intervals (or a 5 in square marked off in 1 in divisions, if you prefer working in inches).

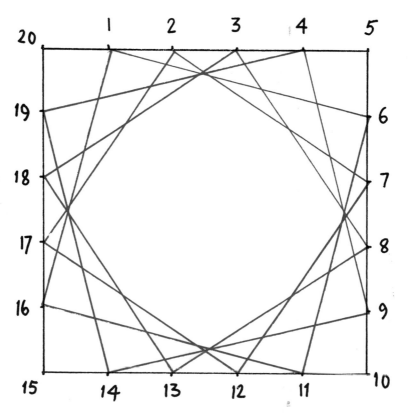

The square on the facing page is formed by joining each point to the one five numbers higher: 1 to 6, 2 to 7, 3 to 8, and so on. This can be called a *plus five pattern*.

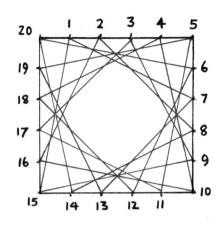

Plus six pattern
Join 1 to 7, 2 to 8, and so on.

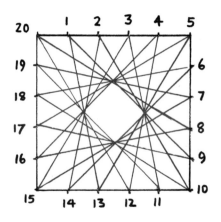

Plus seven pattern
Join 1 to 8, 2 to 9, and so on.

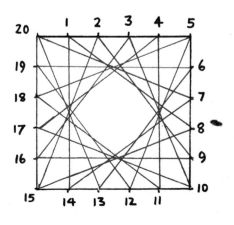

Plus eight pattern
Join 1 to 9, 2 to 10, and so on.

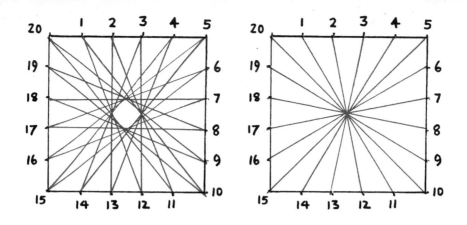

Plus nine pattern (on the left)
Join 1 to 10, 2 to 11, and so on.

Plus ten pattern (on the right)
This is less interesting, but worth remembering in case you want to use this particular design.

Plus more than ten
Try some of these for yourself. You will see that you will be making patterns similar to some you have already done.

A 'plus eleven' pattern looks like a 'plus nine'.
A 'plus twelve' pattern looks like a 'plus eight'.

Using rectangles

Draw a rectangle, its longer sides 10cm and the shorter ones 5cm. Space the points or nails 2cm apart on the longer sides, and 1cm apart on the short ones.

The top one is a 'plus seven' pattern (see page 37). The other is a 'plus nine' (see facing page).

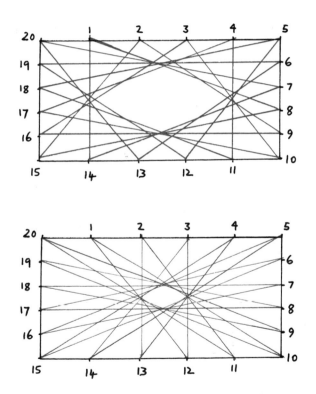

Try varying the measurements of the sides of the rectangle for some of the other patterns. Watch how the patterns change when you do it.

Playing with triangles

Now try experimenting with triangles with sides of different lengths.

Compare this one with the pattern on page 10.

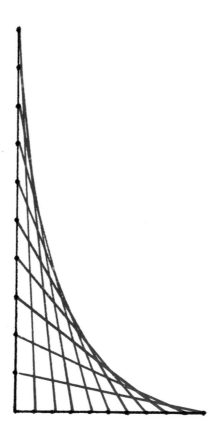

The joins are made in the same order as before. There are still ten points along each arm, and these ten points are equally spaced. The only difference is that one arm is longer than the other.

Reflected triangles

From this you can make a 'reflected' image by placing two triangles back to back.

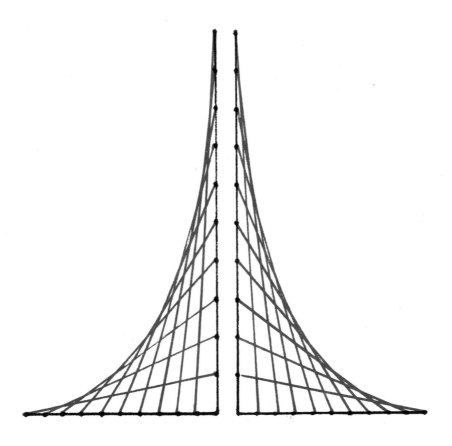

Turn the book upside down and you will see the effect of 'hanging' this pattern from the top, instead of letting it appear to rise from the base line. Turn the page sideways to see the effect this pattern will have then.

Diamond

You could put all four patterns together to make this
diamond effect.

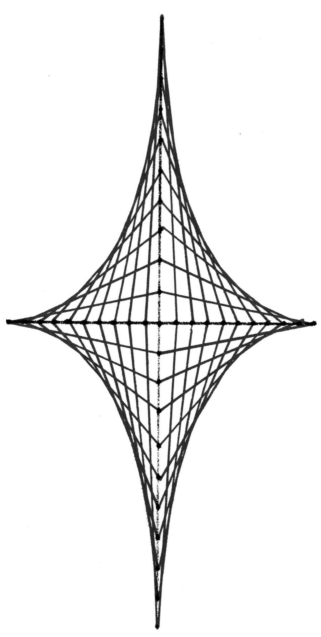

'Inside-out'
If you turn this
shape inside out
and make the
triangle patterns
in the corners,
this is what happens.

Turn the book sideways
to see the effect.

Overlapping triangles

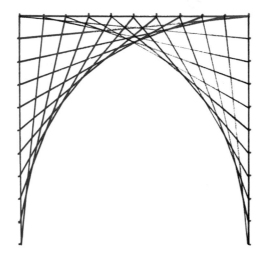

See how you can overlap the patterns if you wish.

You could overlap these patterns inside a triangle. Draw a 60° angle, making the arms the same length and draw in the third side of the triangle. Number the points as shown in the diagram.

Join the points as described on page 9. Then join 11 to 22, 12 to 23, 13 to 24, and so on.

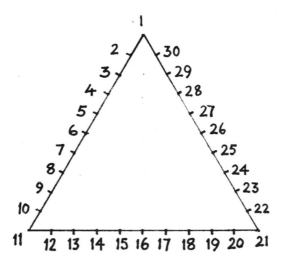

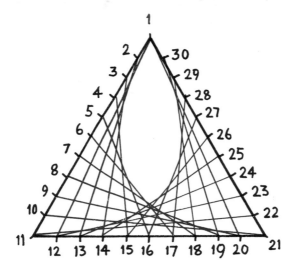

You may like the design just as it is. But if you want to fill in the third angle, these are the points to join.

2 to 21	7 to 26
3 to 22	8 to 27
4 to 23	9 to 28
5 to 24	10 to 29
6 to 25	11 to 30

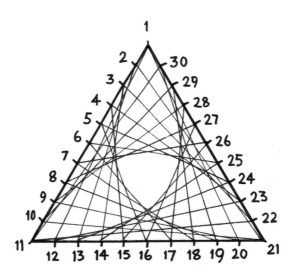

Stretched triangle

You could 'stretch' this triangle as shown below. This one has fifteen points along each axis.

Join 1 to 17, 2 to 18, 3 to 19, and so on to 15 to 31. Continue with 16 to 32 etc to complete the pattern.

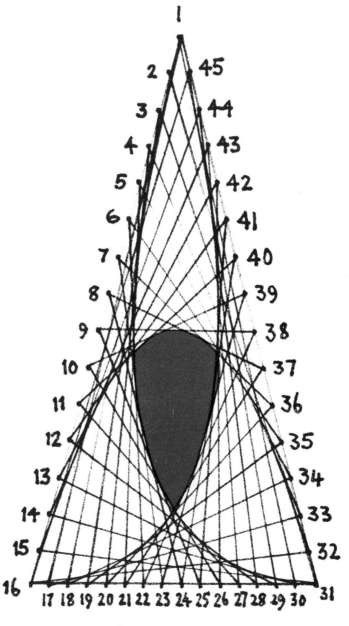

Letter W

You can now go ahead and make up many more designs. This letter M – or letter W, if you use it the other way up – is made up of three triangles.

You could add a butterfly design (see next page) in a second colour.

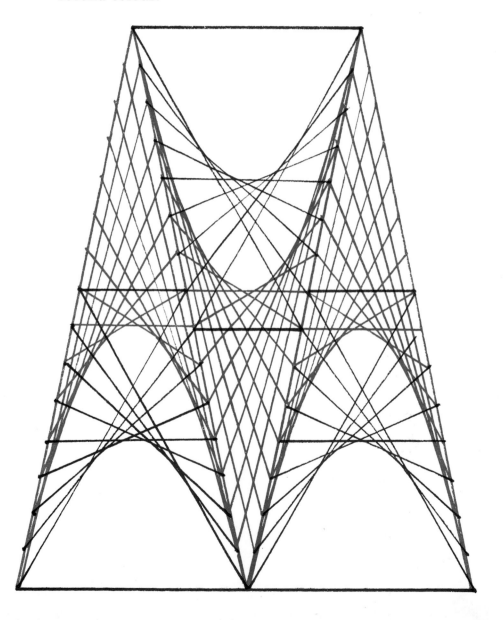

Butterfly patterns

You can make a very simple 'butterfly' pattern using two lines that are not parallel – rather like an angle with the corner missing.

Notice the numbering in the photograph. Each line is numbered from 1 to 21, but you can use as many or as few numbers as you wish. Start the numbering from the top of one of the lines and from the bottom of the other one.

This makes the joins very simple. Join 1 to 1, 2 to 2, and so on.

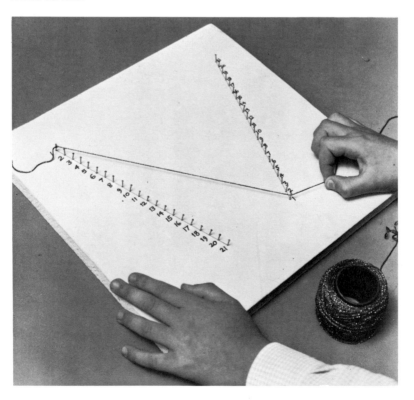

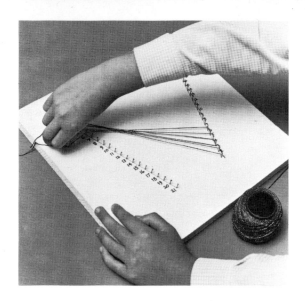

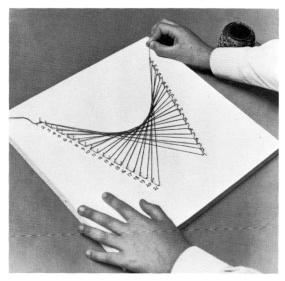

Try the same pattern with a different number of points along the two lines.

Or try it with the lines closer together, or further apart, or at a different angle to each other.

You could also vary the butterfly design by staggering the lines – that is, by drawing the right hand line either higher or lower than the other.

If you draw the two lines parallel, your design will not make a curve as the lines will cross at one point. It will look more like a star than a butterfly.

Opposite : These two designs were made in wire on painted boards. The blue design is made up of two standard butterfly patterns, with staggered butterfly patterns linking the two.
The red design is made up of butterflies in which the two lines almost meet.

Tables the easy way

If you have to learn tables, you may find these patterns will make them more fun.

You need to mark 13 points round the circumference of a circle for the 2, 3, 4, 5 and 6 times tables.

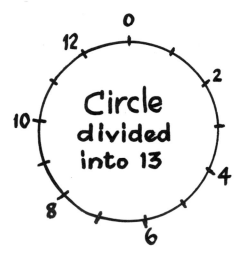

This is how to do it. Use a protractor – a 360° model if you have one. Mark the following degrees: 0, 28, 55, 83, 111, 138, 166, 194, 222, 249, 277, 305, 333. This is not absolutely accurate, but good enough for this purpose.

Opposite : You could make any of the designs in this book on a really large scale. Try one with a group of friends, using string and wooden pegs spaced 0·5 metre apart. These children are pupils at Almond Hill Junior School, Stevenage.

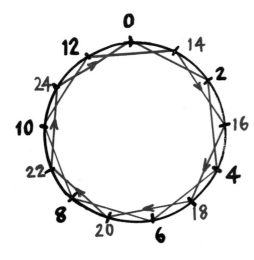

2 times table
Draw a 13-point circle.
Mark in the black numbers.
Join 0 to 2
    2 to 4
    4 to 6
    6 to 8
    8 to 10
    10 to 12

Now the line crosses
over at the top.
What would have been
point 1 now becomes 14,
and so on.
Join 12 to 14
    14 to 16
    16 to 18
    18 to 20
    20 to 22
    22 to 24
Join 24 to 0 to
complete the pattern.

You will see that the
numbers round the circle
are those of the 2 times
table.

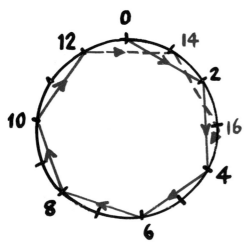

3 times table

Draw a 13-point circle.
Mark in the black numbers.
Join 0 to 3
  3 to 6
  6 to 9
  9 to 12

What would have been
point 2 now becomes 15.
Join 12 to 15
  15 to 18
  18 to 21
  21 to 24

What would have been
point 1 now becomes 27.
Join 24 to 27
  27 to 30
  30 to 33
  33 to 36
and back to 0.

You will see that
the numbers round
the circle are those of
the three times table.

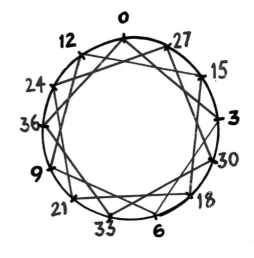

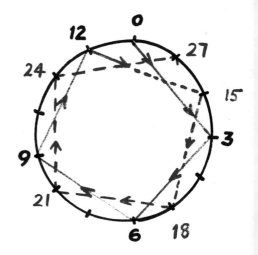

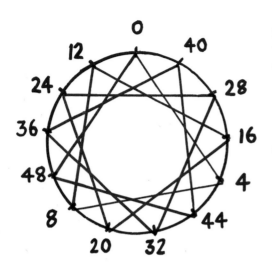

4 times table

Draw the 13-point circle.

Join 0 to 4
      4 to 8
      8 to 12
     12 to 16
     16 to 20,
and so on.

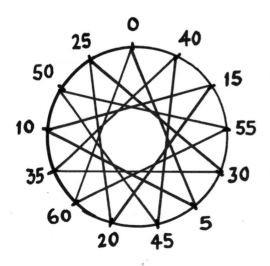

5 times table

Draw the 13-point circle.

Join 0 to 5
      5 to 10
     10 to 15
     15 to 20,
and so on.

6 times table

Draw the 13-point circle

Join 0 to 6
      6 to 12
    12 to 18
    18 to 24,
and so on.

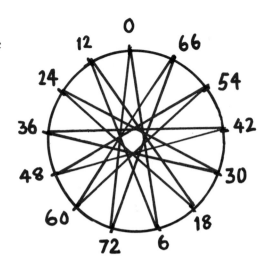

Notice how a different pattern is made by each 'table'.

You can use the 13-point circle for the other tables up to the 12 times table, but you will be repeating some of the patterns you have already drawn. Do you know why?

Combining five patterns

Try drawing the 2, 3, 4, 5 and 6 times tables in the same 13-point circle, one on top of the other. Or make them all on the same nailboard. Or stitch them all on the same tile or piece of card.

You could use a different colour for each table if you want to make it really effective.

7 times table

Use 23, another prime number, as a basis for the 7, 8, 9, 10 and 11 times tables.

Use a 360° protractor to mark off the following angles to make a 23-point circle: 0, 15, 31, 47, 62, 78, 94, 109, 125, 141, 156, 173, 189, 204, 220, 236, 251, 267, 283, 298, 314, 329, 344

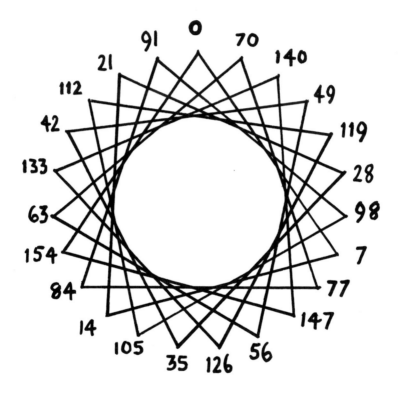

This is the pattern based on the 7 times table. If you start at 0 and follow the line to 7, 14, 21, and so on, you will see how the 7 times table can be built up.

Patterns made from the other tables are just as attractive. Try colouring them in to see the different effects you can produce. And try them one on top of the other using greaseproof or tracing paper or acetate sheet.

8 times table
Add a splash of colour
to your pattern: fibre-tip
pens are ideal for this.

9 times table

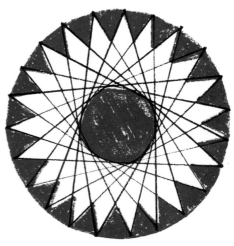

10 times table

59

Making things with the patterns

You can use the patterns in this book for all kinds of
things. Stitched patterns can make very pretty greetings
cards. Try this heart design for a St. Valentine s Day
card.

St. Valentine's Day Card
Draw a 36-point circle.
Join 1 to 2, 2 to 4, 3 to 6, and so on, joining each point
with a number exactly double. Carry on until you reach
18 to 36. Now carry on like this:

19 to 2
20 to 4
21 to 6
22 to 8
23 to 10
24 to 12
25 to 14,
and so on
until you
reach
35 to 34.

Now turn
it upside
down and
you have
a heart.
You could
write your
message
in the
middle.

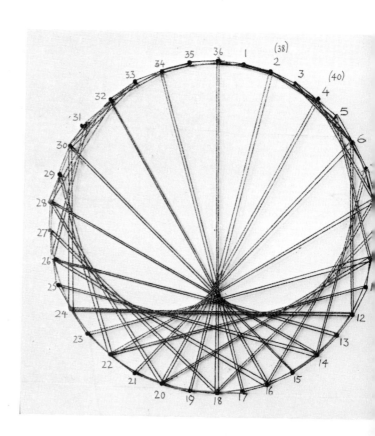

Wall decoration

Any of the designs in the book will look good on a board covered with hessian or felt to blend with the colour scheme of the room.

Aluminium or copper wire or gold or silver lurex thread looks particularly effective under a spotlight or near a window.

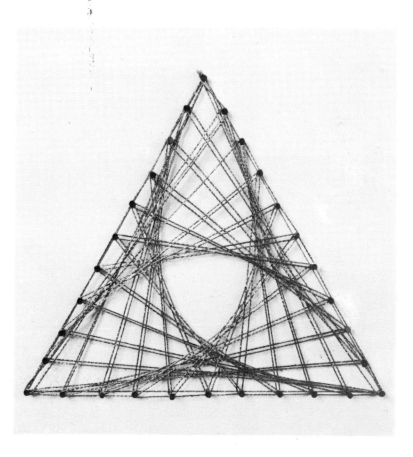

Window pattern
Try a circular pattern on a wooden hoop and hang it in a window.

Glass painting
You could paint one of these patterns on a pane of glass and prop it up in a window for the light to shine through.

Table mats
You could use a design like this for stitching table-mats of card or polystyrene.

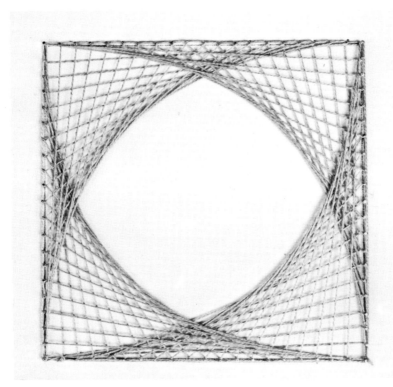

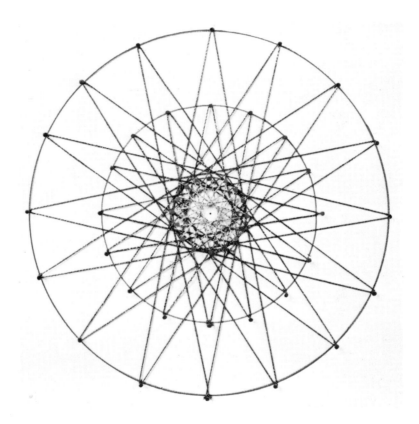

Rug or embroidery designs

You could use these patterns as a design for rug-making or embroidery. Draw the design straight onto the cloth or canvas.

Many circular patterns leave a hole in the middle. When this happens, you can draw two or more designs inside each other.

Supersonic

You could build up some of the patterns you have learned to make pictures or wall hangings.

This plane has a fuselage of card covered with aluminium kitchen foil. The wing, nose and tail patterns are all built up on obtuse angled triangles (see page 11) using silver thread. Wire would have looked good too.

'Supersonic' would look extra effective if you could find or paint a large picture of clouds or open sky to use as a background.

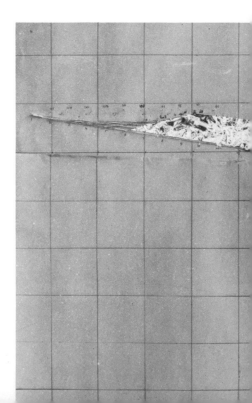

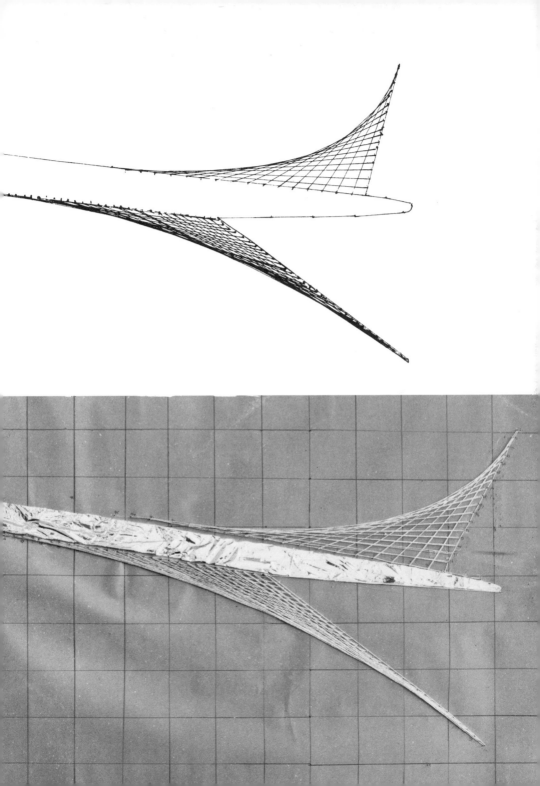

Notes for parents and teachers

Group projects Once they have fully mastered one of the patterns on a small scale, groups of friends may like to try a large outdoor model with string and wooden pegs (see page 52).

Nail-boards (see page 26) If these are to be used repeatedly, perhaps in the classroom, it is a good idea to paint the numbers onto the board after it has been given a coat of emulsion paint.

Six-point circle (see page 18) Older children will be able to draw these with compasses without difficulty. It would be advisable to draw them out for younger children or to let them trace one from the book.

Squares (see page 38) Children should perhaps be left to discover for themselves that 'plus nine' and 'plus eleven' produce identical patterns, as do 'plus eight' and 'plus twelve'. They could then be helped to find out why this is so.

Templates For repeated variations on the same pattern, and also in order to help younger children, you may like to make cardboard templates of some of the more difficult shapes, particularly the multi-pointed circles. Draw out the circle in two or more sizes, as shown, and draw in the angles. Glue the paper onto stiff cardboard and push a compass point through at the points where they intersect. The child may then mark out the points on his own paper by laying the template on top and pricking through the holes with an ordinary pin or point of compasses.

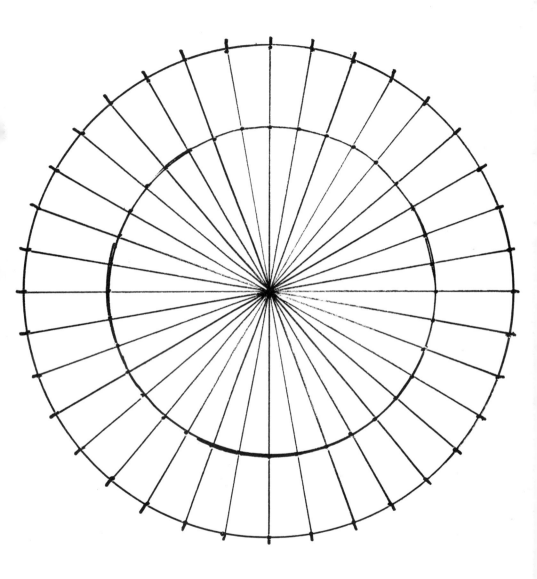

Index